Citizenship

Julie Murray

Abdo Kids Junior
is an Imprint of Abdo Kids
abdobooks.com

Abdo
CHARACTER EDUCATION
Kids

abdobooks.com

Published by Abdo Kids, a division of ABDO, P.O. Box 398166, Minneapolis, Minnesota 55439.

Printed in China

102019

012020

THIS BOOK CONTAINS RECYCLED MATERIALS

Photo Credits: iStock, Shutterstock

Production Contributors: Teddy Borth, Jennie Forsberg, Grace Hansen

Design Contributors: Christina Doffing, Candice Keimig, Dorothy Toth

Library of Congress Control Number: 2019941188

Publisher's Cataloging-in-Publication Data

Names: Murray, Julie, author.

Title: Citizenship / by Julie Murray

Description: Minneapolis, Minnesota : Abdo Kids, 2020 | Series: Character education | Includes online resources and index.

Identifiers: ISBN 9781532188640 (lib. bdg.) | ISBN 9781644942727 (pbk.) | ISBN 9781532189135 (ebook) | ISBN 9781098200114 (Read-to-Me ebook)

Subjects: LCSH: Citizenship--Juvenile literature. | Civics--Juvenile literature. | Community life--Juvenile literature. | Community involvement--Juvenile literature. |

Classification: DDC 323.6--dc23

Table of Contents

Citizenship 4

Ways to be a Good Citizen 22

Glossary. 23

Index 24

Abdo Kids Code. 24

Citizenship

Citizenship is important. It is being part of a **community**.

How can you be a good citizen?

There are many ways.

Jess helps clean the park.

She picks up trash.

Tim fell down.

Ben helps him up.

Mia follows the class rules.

She raises her hand.

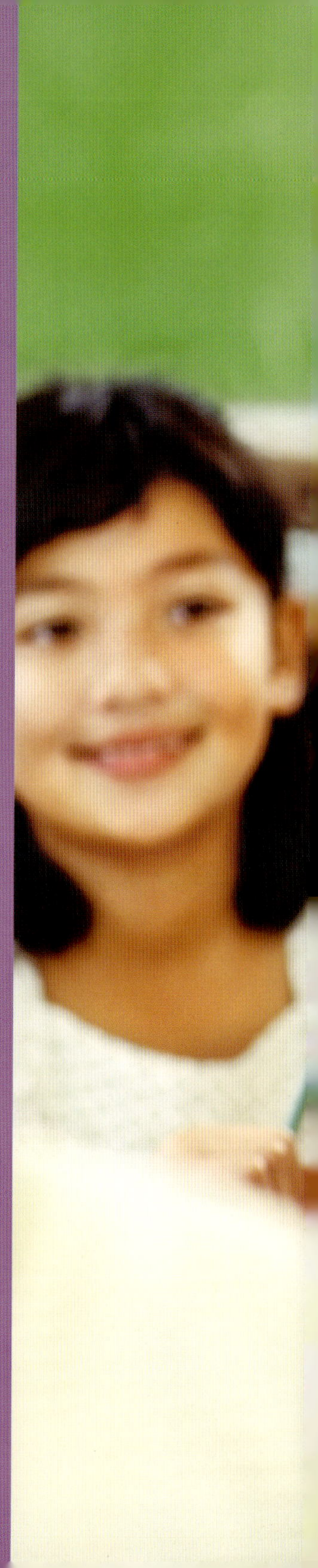

Wes has a lemonade stand. He makes $50. He **donates** it to help others.

LEMONADE
50¢

Kate is done with her bottle.

She recycles it.

Lou helps at home.

He feeds the dog.

Are you a good citizen?

Ways to be a Good Citizen

donate old toys

follow the rules

have a neighborhood party

help others

Glossary

community
a group of people who live close together or have shared interests.

donate
to give in order to help a charity or other group.

Index

charity 14

chores 18

classroom 12

kindness 10

meaning 4

park cleanup 8

pet care 18

recycling 16